Men of the Diesels

H.G. FORSYTHE

Designed by Derek Huntriss
Printed by Century Litho, Penryn, Cornwall
Bound by Booth Bookbinders, Penryn, Cornwall

ISBN 0-906899-31-1

Published by
ATLANTIC TRANSPORT PUBLISHERS
Waterside House   Falmouth Road
Penryn   Cornwall TR10 8BE
England

Atlantic

The Author

H.G. Forsythe is a professional writer, photographer and scientific consultant. He is the author of two highly successful companion volumes in this series, *Steam Shed Portrait* and *Men of Steam*, also published by Atlantic Transport Publishers.

Acknowledgement

The author wishes to express warmest thanks to Mr Jack Gardner, recently retired from British Rail and currently Steam Inspector at the GWS depot, Didcot, and Diesel Inspector for the Severn Valley Railway, for invaluable assistance in compiling this book. Jack Gardner is the author of the book *Castles to Warships* published in 1986 by John Murray.

The Photographs

Thanks are due to the distinguished railway photographers who have provided photographs for this book. The author's own pictures were taken on 35mm film using a Leica IIIf camera.

FRONT COVER: On 23rd June 1988, Class 37 37673 receives attention at St Blazey from Field Support Engineer Paul Holmes from Derby. Major problems with the locomotive's slow running gear were diagnosed and it was despatched to Plymouth Laira tmd for repairs. *Photo: Derek Huntriss*

REAR COVER: HST servicing at Longrock depot, Penzance, on 22nd June 1988.
Top left: Topping up gearbox.
Top right: Checking battery connections.
Bottom left: Checking screen washers.
Bottom right: Refuelling.
Photos: Derek Huntriss

TITLE PAGE: Class 50 50039, based at Old Oak Common, is trapped in the platform and awaits the departure of the 16.55 Newbury service before undertaking other duties. *Photo: Keith Hawkins*

RIGHT: Deltic D9000 (55022 *ROYAL SCOTS GREY*) leaving Edinburgh for Kings Cross with the 16.00 Sundays only departure, diverted via the Edinburgh suburban loop on 4th June 1970. The second man gives a cheery wave to the photographer. This Deltic is one of six to be preserved in addition to the prototype and is at present at Tyseley having spent some time on the Nene Valley Railway at Peterborough. *Photo: J.H. Cooper-Smith*

OPPOSITE: Driver W. Reed of Kings Cross sits comfortably at the controls of Brush Type 2 D5643 as it heads the up Sheffield Pullman in September 1961. The regulator is in the fully open position. *Photo: Author*

Introduction

Back in 1948, when the 4 big railway companies were nationalised and British Railways came into being, there were 19,630 route miles in our railway system and BR employed 641,046 people. In those days steam was supreme, although electrification had taken place in some areas, notably the south east. New steam locomotives were being designed and built and the few examples of diesels which did exist were either prototype experimental machines or were used in shunting.

Within a few years, however, revolutionary changes were to take place. In 1954 the Modernisation Plan was published which proposed the replacement of steam with electric and diesel power. In 1956 the government decided to press ahead rapidly with dieselisation and between the years 1957 to 1968 over 16,000 steam locomotives were removed from service, some almost new, and were replaced by a variety of diesel locomotives. In some areas electrification took place or was extended.

Looking after steam locomotives and keeping them on the road required a veritable army of workers and the work was often dirty and unpleasant. In my books Men of Steam and Steam Shed Portrait, I have described what it was like to maintain and drive steam engines. Because of the unpleasant working conditions in the 40s, 50s and 60s it was becoming increasingly difficult to recruit staff. So the far better working and driving conditions brought about by diesels was one significant reason for replacing steam traction.

In order to keep it running the steam locomotive needed a great deal of attention. It had to make frequent visits to the shed or motive mower depot and required constant attention by both shed staff and its crew. When coming on duty, for instance, there were many jobs driver and fireman needed to carry out and numerous checks that had to be made, some of them very dirty indeed. On a large steam passenger locomotive there were some 60 points which needed oiling before the locomotive moved off from the shed. That steam engine would already have had hours of attention from the shed staff. The fire, for example, would have been lit hours earlier in order to raise steam.

A steam engine would spend only about a third of its time actually working and the rest of its life on shed. Diesels run much longer without attention. In theory, they should operate 23 hours out of the 24, only needing one hour for servicing, although in practice this is rarely achieved, two or three hours being more realistic. This is due to locomotives often having to queue at depots to take their turn for servicing. Nevertheless, in practice one diesel locomotive can do the work previously carried out by three steam engines.

These new practices brought about massive changes on our railways. In steam days, at the end of 1959, there were 470 steam sheds. Today there are only a little over 100 motive power depots. Route miles have shrunk to 10,358. Total staff is now 166,989.

There are many reasons for these changes and the smaller number of staff can be related to a contraction of services and the movement of freight traffic from rail to road, but quite a significant proportion has been due to modern types of motive power requiring far less attention in their day to day running and maintenance than their steam predecessors.

In 1987 British Rail had 2,441 locomotives and some 2,600 diesel multiple unit vehicles. Each machine works a far more intensive schedule than was ever possible with steam traction and to keep them functioning safely and efficiently they still need skilful and careful attention from the railway staff.

Dieselisation brought about a complete revolution in working practices on the railway. Gone were those dark, dirty and smoky sheds and in their place were almost clinically clean stabling points and traction maintenance depots. Drivers enjoy comfortable, warm and clean cabs, a far cry from their roaring, bucking toeholds in the cab of the steam engine, roasted on one side and frozen on the other.

This book takes a look at some aspects of the life of "the men of the diesels". We will go back in time to the days when the diesels were beginning to appear and see what it is like to be a railwayman in charge of today's modern motive power.

Obviously, conditions are vastly better than they ever were in steam days. But are they as rewarding?

H. G. Forsythe

The Prototype Deltic Locomotive

When the prototype Deltic locomotive emerged from the English Electric works at Preston in 1955 it caused a major sensation in railway circles.

The Deltic was unique. Not only was it an entirely private venture on the part of the English Electric Company but the Deltic design was quite revolutionary in its day and the use of two compact and powerful Napier-Deltic opposed piston marine engines enabled it to develop 3,300 horsepower in a locomotive weighing only 106 tons. With a Co-Co wheel arrangement, it was then the most powerful single unit diesel electric locomotive in the world and was to remain so for some years. The English Electric Company had great hopes for overseas sales and so made the prototype rather American in design with headlights at both ends. The much criticised livery of pale blue, cream and gold was very striking. There were "speed wings" at each end and arrowed decorations on either side. The Deltic never carried a running number and had a simple nameplate on each side. The locomotive's striking appearance created attention wherever it went — which was precisely the aim of English Electric.

The prototype Deltic underwent extensive tests on British Railways, although it never passed into direct ownership of BR. It was always accompanied by a team of English Electric engineers.

For some years the Deltic operated out of Euston on the London Midland Region and then, in 1959, moved over to the Eastern Region where on September 2nd of that year I made the footplate trips described here.

On the Eastern Region the locomotive was on a 624 mile roster every day which involved working the White Rose from Kings Cross to Doncaster leaving Kings Cross at 8.50 am returning on the 1.49 pm (the 12.30 pm Hull to Kings Cross) and to Doncaster again on the 8.30 pm mail. The return trip was made with the 1.03 am parcels. The Deltic was refuelled at Kings Cross station depot and some minor servicing was carried out there and at Doncaster station. On Sundays, it visited Hornsey MPD for cleaning and routine maintenance.

On the basis of BR's experience with the prototype, 22 production models were ordered to replace 55 express passenger steam locomotives on the east coast main line.

More than any other locomotive, the Deltics demonstrated the true potential of diesel electric traction on Britain's railways. They became immensely popular with railway enthusiasts and six survive in preservation, in addition to the prototype.

In 1961 the prototype suffered an engine failure and was withdrawn. The English Electric Company returned it to first class condition and then presented it to the Science Museum in London where it arrived on 28th April 1963. Today it can be seen in the railway gallery together with *The Rocket* and the Great Western's *Caerphilly Castle*.

The Science museum would like to replace the Deltic with a more recent example of diesel traction if a suitable home could be found for it. This is difficult to understand because the Deltic was indeed a unique machine, being the very first relatively lightweight but very powerful diesel railway locomotive. Sadly the 22 production Deltics for the Eastern Region were the sum total of these locomotives produced and hoped for export orders never materialised. Just why has never been explained satisfactorily. Possibly the cost was too high to compete with American manufacturers or possibly adhesion problems when hauling heavy loads might have been a disadvantage. After all, under American conditions, a rake of lower powered diesel units would adhere far better to the track than a relatively lightweight single unit. The Deltics have passed into railway history, in their own way just as famous as their great predecessors, the A3s and A4s of the east coast route.

OPPOSITE: The prototype Deltic at the head of the White Rose 8.50 am train to Doncaster at Kings Cross on September 2nd 1959, the day the author made the footplate trip described here.

TOP: View from the cab of the Deltic as she eases the White Rose through Gas Works Tunnel. Dead ahead is the bridge carrying the North London Line and on the left is Belle Isle Junction leading to Kings Cross motive power depot. An A4 Pacific is just coming off shed. Gasworks and Copenhagen Tunnels on their rising grade of 1 in 107 were often damp and greasy, and wheel slipping was very common. Some skill in handling the regulator was necessary to avoid wheel slip and there have been occasions when Deltics have got stuck in the tunnel when attempting to move very heavy trains out of Kings Cross a little too smartly.

BOTTOM: Near Hitchin we passed the down Master Cutler headed by one of the new English Electric Type 4 1Co-Co1 2,000 horsepower diesel electric locomotives. These engines weighed 133 tons compared with the Deltic's 106. They were later reclassified Class 40 and enjoyed great popularity. The class leader D200 has been restored to original condition and has recently joined the National Railway Museum collection at York. All other members of the class have been withdrawn. However, 40106 is preserved on the Great Central Railway and 40145 at the Bury Transport Museum.

From the footplate: Crossing the River Nene bridge just outside Peterborough.

Top Link driver C. Huggins of Kings Cross rests a hand on the Deltic's controller, almost in the closed position as we coasted along at 70 miles per hour. The handle on the right is the train brake.

From the footplate: Mail bag pick-up apparatus at Walton, just outside Peterborough. None of these pick-ups, once so popular, exist today.

Passing Stoke Box at 75 miles per hour. The Deltic regularly flew up Stoke Bank at 90 miles per hour, but that day signals held us back.

From the footplate: Askham Tunnel, only 57 yards long, is a well known landmark for drivers because it marks the halfway point between Kings Cross and Newcastle.

At Doncaster, engine oil was replenished in the platform. Note that the spotter on the left is carrying a gasmask satchel — left over from World War II.

LEFT: The Deltic eases down on the coaches of the 1.49 pm, with station staff ready to couple up.

RIGHT: From the footplate: at Retford, the down Queen of Scots, headed by A1 Pacific 60117 *Bois Roussel*, thunders past the 1.49 pm from Doncaster.

TOP: From the footplate: entering Platform 2 at Peterborough.

BOTTOM: View from the Deltic's footplate as she is just about to emerge from Gasworks Tunnel to enter Kings Cross station.

OPPOSITE, TOP: During refuelling at Kings Cross station depot, English Electric engineers inspect the Deltic's bogie while Inspector Corns poses beside her.

OPPOSITE, BOTTOM LEFT: The station depot at Kings Cross was in 1959 well equipped to deal with diesels. Here the Deltic is having her fuel tanks replenished ready for her next run north with the 8.20 pm mail.

OPPOSITE, BOTTOM RIGHT: On Sundays, the Deltic spent the day at Hornsey mpd for cleaning and routine maintenance. In this picture shed cleaners restore a brilliant shine to the Deltic's blue exterior.

LEFT, TOP: On top of one of the Napier Deltic engines, Mr Smith checks fuel injectors.

LEFT, BOTTOM: Part of the maintenance of the Deltic locomotive was greasing of parts where necessary. In this picture English Electric engineer Mr M J Smith greases the Hardy-Spicer driving shafts to the ventilating fans.

BELOW: Inside the Deltic's main engine room Mr M J Smith checks out one of the 18 cylinder Napier Deltic diesel engines.

ABOVE: Mr Smith inspects one of the Deltic's generators.

LEFT: A cleaner gives special attention to the bogie and brake cylinders.

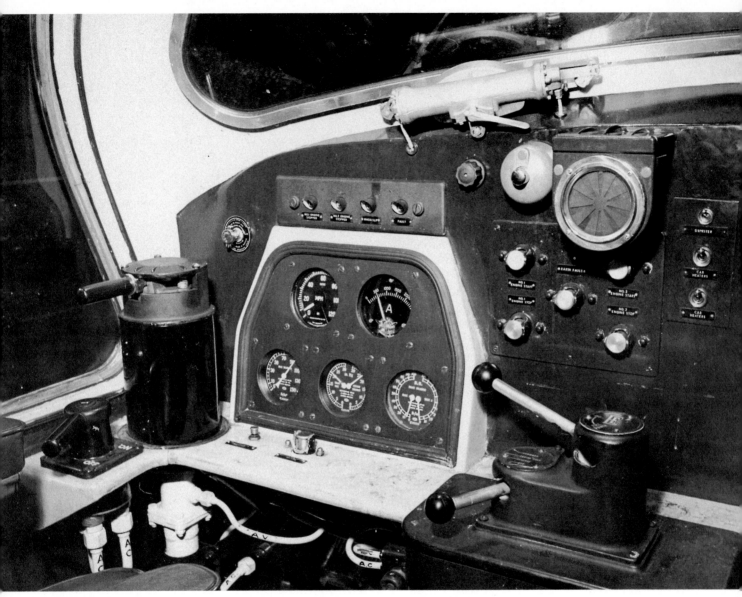

ABOVE: Driver's instrument panel and
controls in production Deltic D9004
photographed at Kings Cross in 1961. The
white painted pipes below the instrument
console are all air pipes, either vacuum or
compressed air.

ABOVE: The author in the cab of the Deltic a few minutes before departure of the White Rose from Kings Cross. The "comb" to the right in front of the cab window was found necessary to break up the smooth airstream and let air enter the radiator openings. *Photo: D.E. Strachan*

BELOW: Front end of the prototype Deltic immediately after arriving at Kings Cross with the 1.49 pm from Doncaster.

Driving, Checking and Minor Servicing

When coming on duty, drivers register in at their depot. Usually, they are then allowed ten minutes or so "walking time" to get to their locomotives; this includes checking the depot notice boards for operating instructions such as speed restrictions.

A driver's locomotive will already have been fuelled, oiled, watered, examined and any minor repairs carried out by the depot maintenance staff. Nevertheless, there are a number of important checks and inspections to be made by the driver before he moves off to pick up his train. These vary with the type of locomotive but will usually last between 20 and 30 minutes. When he reaches his locomotive, the driver will first of all put his personal effects in the cab. Then he will walk round the engine checking everything outside including connecting pipes and cables. If there is a number to be set he will do it now.

Inside the cab, which is the one he will be using for driving, he'll check that isolating cocks are in position, that the fire equipment and protective items such as flags and detonators are all present and correct. In the engine room he will check fuel levels (if he had not done this from outside) and that dip sticks are in place and oil levels and water levels are correct. Next he will check electrical components, particularly the circuit breakers and he will put in the battery switch. This will have been left out by the maintenance staff.

He will then go through to the second cab and check it out in the same way as he had done the first one. From this back cab he will then start the engine. He won't leave until everything is correct and in particular the air pressures are O.K. From the back cab he will do a complete brake test. Then he will shut down the back cab and make sure the AWS (automatic warning system) is shut off. Then he will walk back through the engine room while the engine is running. At this point he will check that there are no leaks anywhere, as pressure has now built up. In the front cab

he will do another complete brake test before moving off. Unlike steam days there is no oiling to be done and no need for the driver to get dirty.

Driving a diesel is vastly different from driving a steam locomotive. For a start the cab is comfortable and warm. Indeed, the driver often enjoys the same standard of comfort as the passengers in the train behind him. In steam days a great deal of skill and experience was required by drivers to get the best out of their locomotives. Adjustment of regulator and cut-off — depending on gradients, loads and other conditions — were necessary and drivers had to be constantly in-tune with their engines. Diesels, however, do most things for you. The driver will set his regulator for the amount of power he requires and the automatic control equipment of his locomotive will do the rest.

Although much is now automated there are some areas where skill in handling locomotives is still necessary. Most notably, in starting, drivers need to avoid wheel slip. This was specially important as far as the Deltics were concerned and some other types, too, are prone to wheel slip.

Knowing the route is just as important for diesel crews as it was for steam engine men but these days it is actually more difficult to know precisely where you are, especially at night. Today's railway is very different from the old. Junction layouts have been simplified, signals are now all the same. The driver is now isolated in the cab from most sounds of the track which were so useful in steam days in identifying exact positions. The steam locomotive would invariably tell its crew when slight changes in gradient occurred, so the crew could instinctively tell where they were. The modern diesel's automatic governing system irons out everything but quite substantial changes. So it is even more important than ever for drivers to be aware of all the topographical characteristics of the route. There are really no problems in daylight but at night small groups of lights, motorways, etc, assume great importance. And when there is a fog at night even greater

Class 50 cab detail

1. Straight air brake valve (locomotive)
2. Train/locomotive brake valve (air/vacuum)
3. AWS 'Sunflower' indicator
4. AWS reset button
5. Air brake pipe pressure gauge
6. Bogie brake cylinder pressure gauge
7. Vacuum pipe/chamber gauge
8. Wheelslip brake button
9. Drivers side window wiper valve
10. Drivers side window washer button
11. Drivers desk illumination dimmer switch
12. Warning horn valve
13. Speedometer
14. Tractive effort pre-set switch
15. Ampmeter
16. Wheelslip indicator light
17. Overload reset button
18. Engine start button
19. Master switch
20. Power controller
21. Slow speed control speedometer
22. Slow speed control setting switch
23. Main reservoir pressure gauge
24. Engine stop button
25. Main fault indicator light
26. Engine stopped indicator light
27. Fire alarm test button
28. Cab ventilation control
29. Cooker control
30. Cooker unit
31. Electric train heat on indicator
32. Electric train heat dimmer switch
33. Electric train heat on button
34. Electric train heat off button
35. Route indicator control handle

concentration is necessary. In steam days drivers could estimate speed very accurately indeed. Every sound, every movement of the steam locomotive told the driver how fast it was moving. And, of course, he was very much exposed in the steam engine cab. In the diesel locomotive, however, the driver is insulated from his surroundings and accurate estimation of speed is very difficult. He must therefore keep a very close eye on the speedometer, far more than was ever necessary with steam traction.

To the outside observer the driver of a diesel may not be such a glamorous figure as the engine driver of an old steam locomotive, but his job is certainly just as fascinating.

RIGHT: View of the driver's side in the cab of D1056 *WESTERN SULTAN* taken at Tyseley in April 1963. The uncomplicated cab layout of the Western Diesel hydraulic locomotives is well illustrated in this shot. These popular locomotives were all withdrawn during the 70s and most were cut up at Swindon Works. No fewer than seven survive in preservation. *Photo: L.C. Jacks*

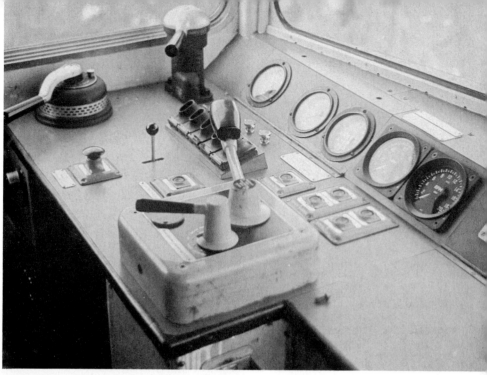

LEFT: Less popular and less reliable were the Warship class diesel hydraulic Type 4 2,200 horsepower locomotives. In this picture a WR driver sits at the controls of a Warship on the road. All the Warships were withdrawn in the late 60s or early 70s. One, D832 *Onslaught* survives and is preserved at Bury Transport Museum. The Warships with Maybach engines were satisfactory machines, but the Warships from number D833 onwards with M.A.N. engines were most unreliable and unpopular. The whole locomotive was regularly filled with fumes. *Photo: L.C. Jacks*

OPPOSITE, TOP LEFT: Driver Trevor Netley of Old Oak Common starts the engines of HST power car 43148 of an Inter-City 125 train bound for the West Country at Paddington on 19th July 1985. *Photo: Keith Hawkins*

OPPOSITE, TOP RIGHT: Driver Bernard Rainbow driving HST 43165 on the 9.50 am Birmingham New Street to York on 11th September 1982. *Photo: L.C. Jacks*

OPPOSITE, BOTTOM: Lineup in Paddington on 19th July 1985. Class 47 47621 *Royal County of Berkshire*, an Old Oak Common locomotive, is in the foreground with a lineup of HSTs. The diesel exhaust fumes caught by beams of sunlight mimic the smoke from former steam days. *Photo: Keith Hawkins*

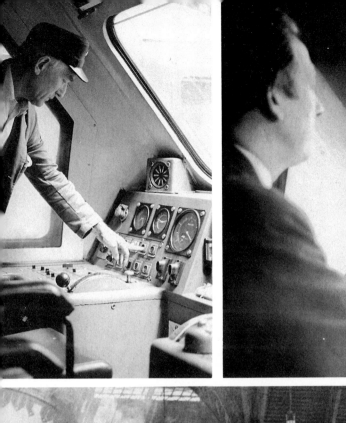

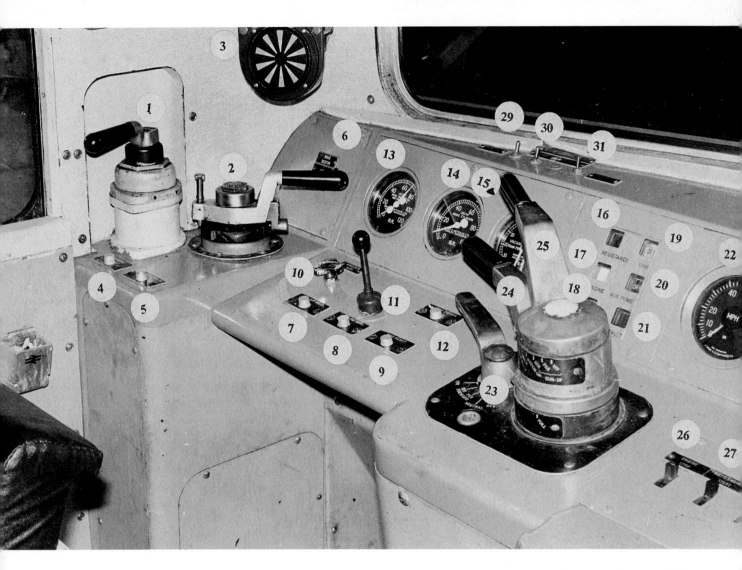

Class 73

ABOVE: These locomotives are particularly interesting as they are designed to operate as electric locomotives on the Southern Region third rail system or as diesel electric engines, and for this purpose are equipped with an English Electric four cylinder RR 600 horsepower diesel engine. It is a simple matter to switch over to either power source.
Photos: Colin J. Marsden

Class 73 and 74 cab layout. Drivers side

1. Straight air brake valve (loco only)
2. Train/locomotive brake valve (air vacuum)
3. AWS Sunflower indicator
4. Sanding push button
5. Exhauster high speed push button
6. Brake selector switch (auto/ep)
7. Anti-slip brake button
8. Rear cab warning horn button
9. AWS reset button
10. Windscreen wiper valve
11. Warning horn valve
12. Shoe down button
13. Main reservoir and train pipe pressure gauge
14. Brake cylinder pressure gauge
15. Vacuum train pipe/chamber gauge
16. Resistance flag
17. Diesel engine prime/start flag
18. Wheelslip flag
19. Line indicator flag
20. Aux power flag
21. General fault flag
22. Speedometer
23. Master switch
24. Diesel power controller
25. Electric power controller
26. Engine stop switch
27. Engine start switch
28. Aux power off switch
29. Demister switch (drivers side)
30. Route indicator light switch
31. Instrument light switch
32. Ampmeter

LEFT: In the equipment room of a Class 47, driver Bernard Rainbow checks the oil dipstick of the locomotive's air compressor.
Photo: L.C. Jacks

RIGHT: Driver L.C. Jacks checking the equipment room, sometimes known as the auxiliary cubicle, of Class 47 47264 at Saltley mpd. This locomotive, originally numbered D1964, was reclassified in August 1984 as 47619. *Photo: L.C. Jacks*

ABOVE: A member of the station staff at Paddington waits for a locomotive to couple up to a rake of Mk I coaches.
Photo: Keith Hawkins

BELOW: At Paddington, Mk I coaching stock is being coupled to a Class 47 locomotive on 19th July 1985. *Photo: Keith Hawkins*

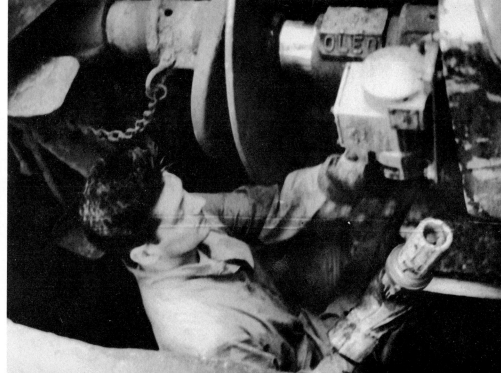

RIGHT: HST 43024 having its windscreen and lamps washed down at Paddington before leaving as the 15.45 service to Penzance from Platform 5 on 12th July 1985.
Photo: Keith Hawkins

LEFT: Drivers chat at Paddington a few minutes before departure. The locomotive on the right is Class 47 47443, based at Crewe.
Photo: Keith Hawkins

ABOVE: At Temple Meads, Bristol, on a freezing, foggy day in February 1975, enginemen walk down the platform before crossing the board walk to Bath Road mpd to clock on for a spell of duty.
Photo: Nigel Trevena

On Shed – At Works

The original Modernisation Plan envisaged the long term replacement of steam traction with electric and diesel power. It provided for a three year test period of a number of makes and types of diesel locomotives and a properly phased transition from steam to other forms of traction, area by area, so that difficulties of steam working side by side with diesels could be avoided. However in 1956 the trial period was abandoned and it was decided to replace steam by diesels as quickly as possible. This was a political expedient and the difficulties caused by diesel locomotives, with their own special servicing requirements, being shedded side by side with steam are now history. Modern diesel stabling points, motive power depots and works are very different from those of steam days.

In early 1987 BR undertook a rationalisation of its maintenance policy for all its traction and coaching stock. Under the new scheme depots and works were to be classified on a scale of 1 to 6 levels, depending on the facilities available and the work carried out at the various locations.

The following is a summary of the services available at each level. *Level 1* is little more than a fuelling point and can provide fuel, oil and water for diesel locomotives together with

very minor servicing. Staff are largely unskilled. *Level 2* servicing facilities are rather better and examination of locomotives can be carried out there. There are facilities for some blocking to be done on brakes. *Level 3* depots

will have facilities for most kinds of examination, maintenance and minor repair work. At *Level 4* there will be the same kind of facilities for maintenance but there will also be provisions for carrying out heavier repairs. There will be cranes, lifting jacks and possibly a wheel lathe. At *Level 5* even heavier repairs can be undertaken and there may be facilities for engine replacement. At *Level 6*, of course, full workshop facilities are available for all kinds of repair.

The allocation of locomotives to specific motive power depots is no longer as important as it was in steam days. Locomotives roam far and wide over the system and can be given attention at depots other than their own. However, they usually return where possible to their allocated depot for repair work of any major kind to be carried out.

ABOVE: Diesel and steam together on shed on 9th May 1959 at Hither Green. On the left is Class 2 Sulzer diesel electric D5003. Close by is Southern Region N class 2-6-0 31852 with C class 0-6-0 31498 on the extreme right. *Photo: R.C. Riley*

LEFT: At Swindon shed on 15th March 1968, D600, the first of the original Warship class has just arrived and is in the hands of North British loco fitters. She was named *Active*. Withdrawn in December 1967 she was cut up at Woodhams, Barry, in March 1970. *Photo: R.C. Riley*

BELOW: Inside a very different Hither Green depot on October 9th 1982, Class 33 diesel electrics 33209 and 33035 are receiving attention. The Class 33 Sulzer engined Bo-Bos, rated at 1,550 horsepower, are particularly liked by enginemen being comfortable, reliable, quiet and efficient. Most of the class still survive although six have been scrapped, most due to accident damage of one sort or another.
Photo: Colin J. Marsden

LEFT: Stewarts Lane is a Level 4 traction maintenance depot. All of the named Southern Region locomotives have been prepared at Stewarts Lane for their naming ceremonies. Here 33056 and 33027 receive final attention on 1st September 1980 prior to their naming at Waterloo the next day. 33056 is *The Burma Star*. The following year she was badly damaged at Earlswood and was out of service until the end of 1982. 33027 was named *Earl Mountbatten of Burma*. Photo: Colin J. Marsden

RIGHT: Another named engine at Stewarts Lane Depot. The staff pose beside electro-diesel 73123 *Gatwick Express* on 9th May 1984 after repainting in "Gatwick Express" livery. Photo: Colin J. Marsden

ABOVE: Brush Class 47 2,580 horsepower Co-Co 47474 receives attention at Ranelagh Yard at Paddington on 22nd July 1978. This large class of locomotives still remains virtually intact. *Photo: Gavin Morrison*

RIGHT: Class 50 50016 *Barham* having her engine oil replenished in Ranelagh Yard at Paddington on 22nd July 1978. The maintenance man on the left is operating a small electric pump delivering oil from the drum through the hose to the locomotive. These English Electric 2,700 horsepower Co-Cos use a lot of oil as can be seen around the vents on the roof. All of the Class 50s were hired to BR when new by English Electric. Later they were bought by British Rail. Most of the Class 50s are still in service but it has been decided that no further heavy repairs will be undertaken.
Photo: Gavin Morrison

TOP LEFT: At Toton traction maintenance depot two Class 45 BR/Sulzer 2,500 horsepower 1Co-Co1 diesel electric locomotives receive attention. 45133 is on the hoist and one of her bogies is seen partially dismantled in the foreground. The housing seen to the right of the bogie is the cover for the main transmission gear. The Class 45s have now been withdrawn although 45060 (D100 *Sherwood Forester*) has been preserved. *Photo: Gavin Morrison*

BOTTOM LEFT: Inside Eastleigh depot. In this picture, taken on 31st October 1981, Class 33s 33105, 33025 *Sultan* and 33116, all belonging to Eastleigh, are receiving attention. 33105 has been lifted off her bogies. Note, at the extreme right, the modern time clock used by staff for checking in and out. This replaced the old fashioned punch time clock which had been there for many years.
Photo: Gavin Morrison

TOP RIGHT: At Gateshead traction maintenance depot, fuelling sheds are provided and on the left a loco washing plant. All locomotives completing a turn of duty are fuelled and washed before proceeding into the shed or storage sidings. *Photo: T.C. Gorman*

OPPOSITE, TOP LEFT: Interior of the cab of Class 47 47523. This is a Gateshead based locomotive and was in for routine maintenance. The cab is in a very messy condition and tape can be seen stuck around parts of the control desk where cracks have appeared and draughts came through.
Photo: T.C. Gorman

OPPOSITE, TOP RIGHT: Roumanian built Class 56 56078, then allocated to Tinsley, was on a visit to Gateshead on 6th July 1985. Although 56078 was a much newer loco than 47523, the cab is in a very scruffy condition.
Photo: T.C. Gorman

OPPOSITE, BOTTOM: Scottish Class 37 37401 is getting some attention at Eastfield Depot in Glasgow on 9th July 1985. These locos are a numerous class with the Co-Co wheel arrangement and are of 1,750 horsepower. Only one has been scrapped and that was in 1965 when D6983 was condemned after an accident. 37401 has been named *Mary Queen of Scots*.
Photo: Gavin Morrison

ABOVE: Doncaster Works, in steam days, was covered in my book *Steam Shed Portrait*. Today's Doncaster is a very different place. In this picture taken on 28th February 1982 two Class 37s are undergoing heavy repair and their nose end valance/route box indicators have been modified. On the left is 37250, then based at Gateshead. On the right is 37200, allocated to Thornaby. *Photo: Colin J. Marsden*

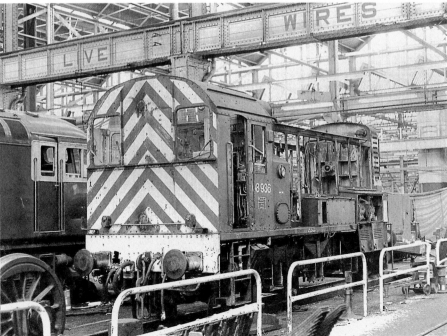

TOP LEFT: Class 27 27002 is receiving attention at Swindon Works on 19th September 1984 although she was withdrawn from service in 1986. Next to her, in a forlorn state, is Class 47 47230 which has obviously suffered collision damage. Although 47230 was repaired and re-entered service she has also since been withdrawn.
Photo: Derek Brown

BOTTOM LEFT: At Swindon Works, Class 08 shunter 08936 is seen extensively stripped down in the early stages of a heavy overhaul on 19th September 1984. *Photo: Derek Brown*

ABOVE: Railway workshops today have the most extensive facilities for diesel repair. Not so perhaps in 1963 when this photograph of D1736 was taken at Swindon Works showing it being lifted by a travelling crane for a bogie change. *Photo: Colin J. Marsden*

Old Oak Common

Old Oak Common depot was opened in 1906 and at that time was the largest Great Western Railway motive power depot. It measured 444 feet by 360 feet and had four 65 foot turntables. Each had 28 radiating roads and there was a total of 112 engine pits. All this was under cover.

On the eastern side of the depot there was a lifting and repair shop which had twelve pits with a traverser outside. My visits to Old Oak Common in steam days are described in *Steam Shed Portrait*. At the end of 1959 Old Oak Common had an allocation of 160 steam engines and 7 diesels.

Today, Old Oak Common is a Level 4 traction maintenance depot for both locomotives and High Speed Trains. The allocations at the end of 1987 were 56 diesel locomotives, and at the nearby HST depot nine HST sets which, of course included 18 power cars. The locomotives included nine Class 08 shunters, five Class 31 diesel electrics, 25 Class 47 diesel electrics and 17 Class 50s.

The great covered steam shed has been demolished and only one of the four turntables remains, this now being out of doors. No trace remains of the old coaling plant. The depot is situated about three miles from Paddington on the up side of the line. The HST depot is about half a mile further on. The photographs in this section were taken by Richard Lewis on Thursday 27th June 1985, except where otherwise credited.

BELOW: The approach to Old Oak Common Depot is very little changed since steam days.
Photo: Richard Lewis

RIGHT: A view of the one remaining turntable at Old Oak Common. The buildings on the right are part of the electrical maintenance shed while to the left is the servicing shed.
Photo: Richard Lewis

LEFT: A view of the servicing shed where diesels are refuelled. The two Class 50s in the picture are 50050 *Fearless* and 50035 *Ark Royal* seen on 12th September 1984.
Photo: Derek Brown

RIGHT: At Old Oak Common. In the immediate foreground, the coaling stage for steam locomotives once stood. The shed on the right is used for underframe cleaning and the building in the background is part of the 'Factory', formerly the repair shops of steam days. The Factory is able to carry out quite major repairs which otherwise might have been undertaken at works.
Photo: Richard Lewis

BELOW: An HST power car stands jacked up in the Factory at Old Oak Common on 12th May 1980 during a bogie overhaul. Unusually, the bogie is still attached to the body.
Photo: Colin J. Marsden

LEFT: Class 47 47286 receives attention to her bogies in the loco jacking area of the Factory. *Photo: Richard Lewis*

BELOW: Inside the engine compartment of Class 47 47500 *GREAT WESTERN*. *Photo: Richard Lewis*

ABOVE: One of Old Oak's Class 50s, 50036
Victorious, receiving major engine repair in
the Factory on 22nd April 1983.
Photo: Colin J. Marsden

DMUs

Diesel multiple units have been around since the early days of modernisation. They have taken the place of many secondary steam services and at first they were greeted with mixed feelings by enthusiasts. Passengers, though, soon discovered that marvellous views were usually available at each end of the unit, the large glass windows enabling them to see into the driver's cab and through his windows. Many a driver has been roundly cursed when he had the temerity to draw the blind between him and the passenger compartment.

DMUs are divided into two main types. There are those fitted with an under floor engine and mechanical transmission and those fitted with an engine room and diesel engine driving a generator producing electrical power for traction bogies.

In 1985, there were nearly 3,000 DMU cars on BR's register. However, many of the original cars dating back to the late 50s and early 60s have come to the end of their useful lives and are rapidly being withdrawn, to be replaced by four-wheel Railbuses, Sprinters and Super Sprinters. Big changes are afoot in the DMU field.

RIGHT: Typical view from a DMU at Workington on a seasonal July day in 1979.
Photo: Nick Stanbra, Atlantic Collection

LEFT, TOP: At Reading, a DMU waits to depart with an Oxford service on 27th July 1985. *Photo: Keith Hawkins*

LEFT, BOTTOM: In a DMU on the Reading to Gatwick route, on 27th July 1985. *Photo: Keith Hawkins*

BELOW: A Southall driver waits in the cab of his DMU at Paddington just before leaving with the 16.05 service to Slough. *Photo: Keith Hawkins*

The driver of a DMU puts the brake handle in at the driving end of the unit. *Photo: Keith Hawkins*

On the Gatwick to Reading service the driver takes advantage of a quiet stretch of line to fill his pipe. *Photo: Keith Hawkins*

RIGHT: Again on the Gatwick to Reading DMU service the driver applies the brake just north of Aldershot. *Photo: Keith Hawkins*

LEFT: On the same service, the DMU approaches Ash. *Photo: Keith Hawkins*

LEFT: The DMU is almost at Reading.
Photo: Keith Hawkins

LEFT: On the return journey from Reading to Gatwick we are now looking out of the back cab of the DMU. Note the brake handle is in the bracket provided for it on the window frame above the AWS flag. In this picture the DMU has just left Wokingham going towards Guildford. The junction in the picture off to the right is the line to Staines. *Photo: Author*

...shot out of the back cab of the ...he Reading to Gatwick service. The ...riving at Guildford and has just run ...bank from Pinks Hill. *Photo: Author*

RIGHT: A DMU climbs the 1 in 37 grade from Exeter St Davids to Exeter Central whilst working the 13.51 service to Exmouth on 8th March 1980. *Photo: Gavin Morrison*

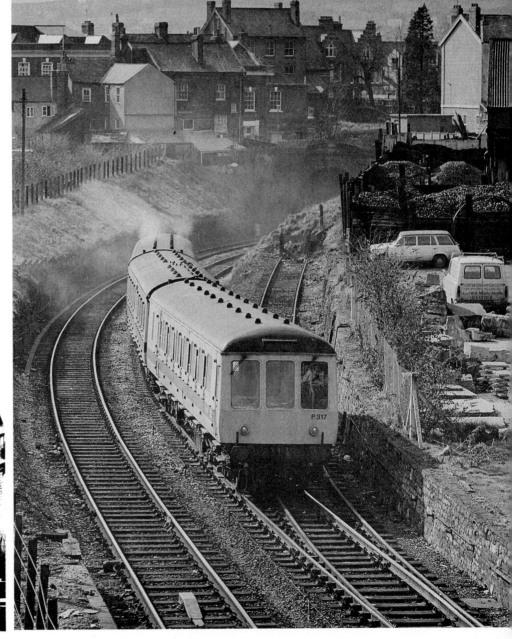

Trip on a Brush Type 2

The Pilot Scheme under the Modernisation Plan called for initial orders of a number of different types and makes of diesels, both diesel electric and diesel hydraulic.

Some of the Pilot Scheme diesels were highly successful and repeat orders were placed by the then British Transport Commission. Many continue to give sterling service today. Others did not survive, some being considered outright failures.

Amongst the most successful of the pilot scheme diesels were the mixed-traffic locomotives built by the Brush Traction Company. They were designated Type 2 and were of 1,250 horsepower with a A1A-A1A wheel arrangement. Twenty were ordered under the pilot scheme and eventually a total of 225 were constructed.

Under the TOPS renumbering scheme they became Class 31. Most of the first 20 have now been withdrawn and scrapped but the class leader 31018, formerly D5500, has been restored to original condition and is preserved at the National Railway Museum.

In September 1961 I had the opportunity to travel in the cab of production model Brush Type 2 D5643 between Grantham and Kings Cross on one of the Sheffield Pullman expresses. This train was scheduled to depart from Sheffield at 3.20 pm with stops at Retford, Grantham and Peterborough. Arriving at Kings Cross at 6.15 pm, the departure from Grantham was scheduled for 4.27 pm.

As I had travelled down to Grantham that day on the footplate of A4 Pacific *Silver Link*, the contrast between the footplate ride on the steam locomotive and the quiet, luxurious comfort of the Brush was quite staggering. It would be true to say that the driver enjoyed virtually the same standard of comfort as a passenger in a first class coach. Conversation was easy and little more than a purr of the diesel engines could be heard even at maximum speed. The following photographs were taken on that trip.

At Peterborough, with steam still very much in evidence.

ABOVE: As D5643 approaches the Hadley Wood Tunnels, two diesels on down trains burst out of the tunnel mouth and are momentarily framed in D5643's cab window. The nearest locomotive is one of the Pilot Scheme English Electric Baby Deltics. These 1,110 horsepower Bo-Bos used one Napier Deltic marine engine similar to the kind that were used in pairs in the Deltics. The high speed diesel engine offered no advantage in Type 2 diesels and indeed proved very troublesome in practice. The Baby Deltics spent a good deal of time out of service and the English Electric Company refurbished the engines over a two year period. None was reordered and all had reached the scrapheap by the late 60s and early 70s. The furthest locomotive here is another of the highly successful Brush Type 2 diesel electrics, a sister of D5643.

LEFT: D5643 arriving at Kings Cross with the up Sheffield Pullman a couple of minutes ahead of time. The train is about to emerge from Gas Works Tunnel and the station platforms are seen here framed in the windscreen.

RIGHT: The Sheffield Pullman has arrived in the platform at Kings Cross station. Driver Reed and his second man are in the cab, while posed alongside is the ER inspector who accompanied me on the journey. D5643 was renumbered 31218 under TOPS.

ABOVE: Survivor and non-survivor, Class 31 31292, still operating out of Bescot, hauls defunct Deltic 55012 (D9012) *CREPELLO* away from Finsbury Park for the last time on 20th May 1981. *CREPELLO* was broken up at Doncaster Works in September of that year. *Photo: Gavin Morrison*

Epilogue

In the early 60s the diesels replaced the beloved steam locomotive. Those same diesels are themselves today being replaced either by electric traction or by new updated diesels.

For many enthusiasts the diesel had become even more interesting than the steam engine. Steam, of course, still has its following but there are many enthusiasts today who have never seen a steam locomotive operating in normal traffic, let alone what it was like in a steam shed. Some diesels have become extremely popular and the Deltics enjoyed a following every bit as enthusiastic as those who loved the A3 and A4 steam Pacifics.

Once again the traction scene is changing making railways just as interesting for the dedicated railway enthusiast as they always were.

BELOW: The driver of Class 47 47447, based at Crewe, settles down to a fairly long wait before departure in Paddington station on 20th July 1985. *Photo: Keith Hawkins*